100 QUESTIONS AND ANSWERS TO HELP YOU LAND YOUR DREAM ANDROID JOB

OR TO HIRE THE RIGHT CANDIDATE!

ENRIQUE LÓPEZ-MAÑAS

INTRODUCTION

There is a boom in the mobile applications market. It has been projected that by the end of 2015 more than a billion (with b) smartphones will be sold, twice as many as the number of personal computers[1]. Mobile channels are increasing their revenue figures, with growth percentages over 100% being the norm and not the exception. Each business needs a mobile application, and therefore the demand for engineers, UX designers and QA testers is rapidly increasing. There are far more jobs than available talent, and the situation is particularly optimistic for senior developers.

If you are reading this book, you likely know the two main fighters of this battle, Android and iOS. They both accumulate up to 90% of the market share[2], leaving the other competitors with a testimonial piece of the global cake. Whereas the market revenue figure was

---

[1]

http://www2.deloltte.com/content/dam/Deloitte/global/Documents/Technology-Media-Telecommunications/gx-tmt-pred15-one-billion-smartphone.pdf

[2] https://www.netmarketshare.com/operating-system-market-share.aspx?qprid=8&qpcustomd=1

traditionally favorable to iOS, this is rapidly changing[3], and Android is taking over Cupertino thanks to its dominance in the emerging markets. Moreover, the predictions are that this gap will increase in the future.

Therefore, If you are already a mobile developer, congratulations! (double congratulations if you are an Android developer!). When I started back in 2008, the version 1.0 of Android was already released 3 years after the Apple counterpart. At that time there was little information and documentation of the API, tutorials were sparse and the community was just starting. Nothing was clear at that time of what could be done with the new Operating System that Google was releasing, and although some of us knew that something big was growing, the entire world was expecting to see its development before betting strongly on Android.

7 years later, the situation has enormously changed. From a lack of information scenario we moved into a too-much-information one. There is a huge community that is regularly contributing to the Android ecosystem with Open Source libraries, tutorials and forums. There is outdated information co-existing with the newest Android trends, and for a newcomer it might be hard to distinguish between them (does it make a lot of sense to

---

[3] http://techcrunch.com/2015/04/14/revenue-gap-between-ios-and-android-apps-grows-thanks-to-china/#.4utbsc:krzm

learn about pure database management having so many ORM frameworks? Should I learn how Maven is working rather than diving in purely Gradle?).

My purpose with this book, as a person that has been both behind and in front of an interview, is to collect and present on a readable way questions and tips on how you should prepare for an Android interview. This book is valid both for interviewers and candidates.

I have also noticed that many of the questions asked at interviews are repetitive, and if you google something like "android interview questions" the same set is always returned. Although those they are still valid, if you are aiming at hiring a senior developer you should consider more advanced questions about architecture, patterns and frameworks.

Each question is answered with a comprehensive and clear reply. Some of the questions provide a bonus, which is typically a topic you want to deep into to further analyze the knowledge of a candidate.

Questions are divided into basic, intermediate and advanced ones. Some people will argue that I could have done two divisions rather than three, but I consider important to have this intermediate category. There are many developers that have been digging for a while into Android, but they have not yet had the time or opportunity to work with more advanced topics. The classification is merely subjective and it is based on my previous experience, but it has been proven useful in my experience as a candidate and an interviewer.

Questions do not always include full coding examples. The purpose of this book is not to be a full guide to the Android API – if you want to know all the details about the Android Permissions or the different types of Content Providers you can always read the Android Developers Page. This book is intended to provide a comprehensive guide in natural language to be used when interviewing a candidate. I also believe that a candidate should not know by heart all the details of a particular API, but articulate it coherently and discuss problems highly abstracted of the implementation details.

The most advanced questions not only include topics from Android, but also programming patterns, architectural design or memory management. A senior developer must be able to use correct strategies to develop a complex application that solves a particular problem, and a purely theoretical knowledge will not be enough to carry this task. A senior engineer needs to be familiar with several Java notions, have practical experience with them and be able to design its own solutions.

These questions have been collected and updated through several years, and being adapted with each

Android release (which happens quite often). I am always glad to receive any feedback that can help me to improve and benefit other people.

This book includes references to commercial software. I am not affiliated to any of these companies, and when the trademark has been registered I will always indicate it. I will always provide an open source alternative to any commercial software, but in some cases it would be fool to ignore a product just because the company is making profit of it.

8

ABOUT THE AUTHOR

Enrique is a Google Developer Expert, and Freelance Mobile Engineer normally based in Munich, Germany (although is hard to catch him up there for more than a few weeks). He develops software and writes about it for money and fun. He spends his free time developing OpenSource code, writing articles, learning languages or taking photographies. He loves nature, beer, traveling, and talking about him in third person.

You can contact him on @eenriquelopez at Twitter, at +EnriqueLópezMañas in G+ and write to him at eenriquelopez@gmail.com

THANK YOU

Many people made this possible.

Personal thanks to Udayan Banerji and your great job reviewing the entire book. This project owes you a lot of its essence. Thanks to the direct reviewers and contributors of the book: César Valiente, Marius Budin, Jose Luis Ugía, César Díez, Alberto Calleja, Jorge Barroso, Nick Skelton. You guys rock.

Thanks to the amazing crew of the Google Developer Expert program. I wake up every day inspired by your daily job, and this book is also the result of many decisions taken where you had a direct influence. Thanks also to my colleagues at Sixt: it has been three unforgettable years working with you, where I have learned many things and grew professionally and personally.

Last but not least, thanks to all my fantastic friends and family, who influence me profoundly. I love you all.

TABLE OF CONTENTS

CHAPTER 3. WE NEED THAT GUY ON BOARD, WE WANT TO DO GREAT THINGS! 79

Chapter 1. Get a Junior Developer

The set of questions presented in this chapter are basic Android questions. Senior developers should be very comfortable answering these, and junior developers, with up to one year of experience, should have knowledge of these concepts.

Question 1: What is an Activity in Android?

An `Activity` can be understood as a screen that performs a very particular action in an Android application (for example, we use an `Activity` to login to or to modify our profile). The activities interact with the user, they present a window and present an interactive UI inside (this is done through the function `setContentView()`). Activities are typically full-screen, but can also be floating screens. They have their own cycle, and are piled within a stack of Activities handle by the operating system

QUESTION 2: CAN YOU EXPLAIN ME HOW THE LIFECYCLE OF AN ANDROID ACTIVITY WORKS?

The Activities are handled in a stack of Activities. Every time an Activity is pushed into the screen, is added to the stack as the first element. When an Activity is destroyed or dismissed, the previous Activity in the stack is presented on the screen.

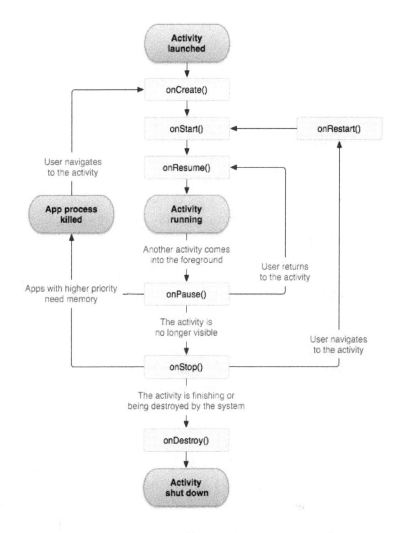

Image obtained from http://developer.android.com/

There is only one `Activity` in running state, and this is the `Activity` being presented on the screen. There are a few more relevant states:

-onPause(). When an Activity loses the focus but is still visible, it moves into the onPause() status. This Activity maintains its state and remains attached to the screen, but the system can kill it if there is a situation of extremely low memory.

-onStop(). This state is the same as onPause(), but the Activity is not visible anymore. The system can also kill it in low memory situations.

-onDestroy() happens when the Activity has been killed by the system or finished by the user. All the information is lost in this state.

-onCreate(). First state of an Activity. All the initialization starts here, and there is also a Bundle object provided to restore previous state if needed.

-onResume(). When the Activity moves from the background into the foreground, the method onResume() is called. Note that this is also called the first time the Activity is created after onCreate()

-onStart(). This method is called when the Activity is first presented to the user.

QUESTION 3: WHAT IS A FRAGMENT? WHY WERE THEY INTRODUCED?

Fragments were first introduced in version 3.0 of Android, as a way to deal with new devices coming into the market (tablets). They provide a modular mechanism to create UI that can be easily reused throughout an application.

As the previous versions of Android only allowed to have one running `Activity`, it was not possible to make use of the entire screen and present different modules on it (a common use-case in tablets was to present a list on one side of the screen, and update the content dynamically on the other side). With this new approach, several fragments could be embedded in an `Activity`, making an application much more interactive.

QUESTION 4: HOW DOES THE LIFECYCLE OF FRAGMENTS WORK?

Fragments do have their own lifecycle, and it is somewhat similar to the lifecycle of Activities. Fragments are attached to Activities and therefore also depend on them (if an `Activity` dies, so does the `Fragment`).

However, as opposed to the Activities, several Fragments can be in a running state at the same time.

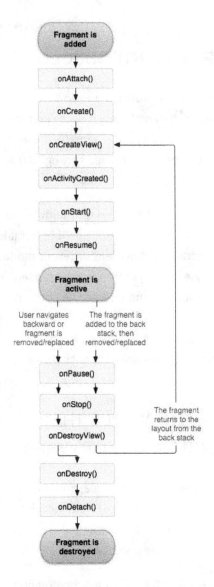

Image obtained from http://developer.android.com/

-onAttach(). This method is called when a Fragment has been successfully attached to an Activity.

-onCreate(). Similar to the Activity, this method is first triggered when the Fragment is first created. In this method we typically initialize the components of the Fragment.

-onCreateView(). When the view hierarchy that has been associated with a Fragment is created, the method onCreateView is called.

-onActivityCreated(). After the method onCreate() of the Activity has been called, this method is also called in the Fragment. Is useful when you have an architecture communicating between both instances (something you will likely have)

-onStart(). As with the Activity, when the Fragment is presented to the user the method onStart() will be triggered.

-onResume(). At this stage, the Fragment is already on the screen and running. This is generally connected to the onResume() method of the Activity.

-onPause(). This state is tied to the onPause() from the Activity, meaning that the `Fragment` is no longer resumed.

-`onStop()`. The `Fragment` is no longer visible. This is also connected to the `onStop()` from the `Activity`.

-`onDestroyView()` is called when a view has been detached from the fragment

-`onDestroy()`. The `Fragment` has been destroyed and is no longer in use.

-`onDetach()`. The `Fragment` has been detached from the `Activity`.

QUESTION 5: WHAT IS THE STRUCTURE OF AN ANDROID APPLICATION?

Please keep in mind that this explanation is specific to Android Studio. Although Android Studio shares many features with other IDEs, it also has its differences (I also think Android Studio/Intellij brings more advantages to a company than an outdated IDE).

In Android Studio, a recently created application contains several modules, one of them being the main application, and others being the libraries. Overall, an Android application contains the following key folders and files:

-**assets**: this folder contain different resources such as databases, text files, etc.

-**build**: this folder is where all the temporary files are deposited before the application actually compiles. It is removed after a clean operation and renewed with each new build.

-**libs**: when there are libraries in individual packages (normally you will deal with .jar libraries) they are included in this folder. Note that this is not a technical requirement, but a de-facto standard.

-**src**: all the source files are within this folder. This folder is divided in the subfolders main/java (which includes the source code) and main/res (which includes the android resources).

- **build.gradle**: this file includes information about how to build the application.

- **AndroidManifest.xml**: the Manifest in Android handles essential information that the system needs to run application. Some of this information includes:

> - Components of the application. All the Activities, Services, Broadcast Receivers and Content Providers need to be defined in the Manifest.

> - Permissions that the application must have in

order to access system functions.

- Instrumentation classes.

Some of the functionality of the Manifest has been moved to the build.gradle file (such as declaring minimum API version or versionCode).

QUESTION 6: WHAT ARE THE PERMISSIONS IN AN ANDROID APPLICATION?

The permissions, specified in the *AndroidManifest.xml*, declare which functionality of the system an application can access. These permissions are declared at installation time, and they cover a wide range of functionality:

- Access the camera

- Perform Internet connections

- Access the Location hardware of the device.

- Making usage of the NFC hardware.

- Accessing the sensors

- Dialing a phone number

At the time of writing this book (June 2015) the

Developer Preview of the Android M[4] version includes
runtime permissions. Whether this new feature will be
included in the release version of Android M remains a
mystery, and this section might need to be updated in
future releases.

QUESTION 7: WHAT IS AN INTENT? HOW MANY DIFFERENT INTENT TYPES YOU KNOW?

An `Intent` is a message sent between Android
components to request functionality and interactions
between them. An `Intent` can be used not only to
access different components of an application, but also
to interact with different applications (for example, an
Intent can call another application to take a picture, and
retrieve it for the calling application).

A very common use for an `Intent` is to start different
Activities within an application.

There are two main types of Intents:

EXPLICIT INTENTS

An explicit Intent defines exactly which component we

4

https://developer.android.com/preview/features/
runtime-permissions.html

want to call in the Android system. The most common use is to open another `Activity`.

```
Intent intent = new Intent(this,
SecondActivity.class);

startActivity(intent);
```

IMPLICIT INTENTS

An implicit `Intent` does not specify which component will take over the next action, but instead it indicate the action that must be performed. The Android system will search for a set of components that can perform the action (for instance, dialing a phone number) and present them in a selection screen to the user.

QUESTION 8: HOW CAN I PERSIST INFORMATION IN AN ANDROID DEVICE?

Android applications need to persist and save information in the device memory. The more non-trivial an app becomes, the more information and more complex information it needs to store and handle.

Natively, Android provides three different methods to persist information:

SHAREDPREFERENCES

The API `SharedPreferences` allows the app to save a set of Key-Values in the application data folder. This is generally used to save small collections, such as personal preferences. The resulting file is saved as an XML file within the application folder (/data/application.package).

SQL DATABASE

In Android we can make use of SQLite Databases to store structured data, or information that is more complex than a key-value set. The package android.database.sqlite provides the necessary API to perform the operation.

> There are ORM libraries that can abstract this operation and make the process easier. A candidate knowing some of these frameworks shows a deeper knowledge

FILES

Files are used to handle a big amount of data (for example, image files). These files can be saved in the internal storage (accessible from the current application) or in the external storage (accessible from the entire system). An Android application persisting information in external files needs to declare the permission *WRITE_EXTERNAL_STORAGE*.

QUESTION 9: WHAT IS A SERVICE IN ANDROID, AND HOW MANY TYPES OF SERVICES DO YOU KNOW?

A `Service` is a component that performs long-running operations in the background, and does not have an interface. Services are started by other application component, and they remain running in the background whether the other component remains active or not.

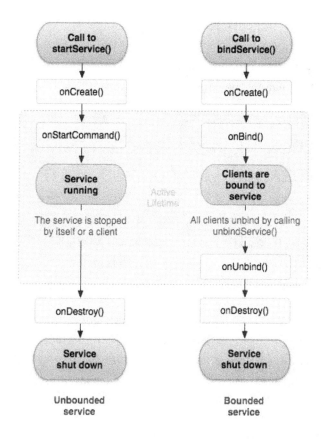

Image obtained from http://developer.android.com/

Similar to the Activities and Fragments, the services have their own lifecycle. A Service can be either Bounded or Unbounded. A Bound service is connected to another componen, and it typically lives while the other component is still alive. By calling the functions bindService() or unbindService() the service will be bound/unbound from the component.

A service that has been started with the `onStartCommand()` function will be unbounded from any other component, and will keep running indefinitely, even if the component that started it is destroyed.

QUESTION 10: WHAT IS A CONTENT PROVIDER, AND WHAT DO YOU USE IT FOR?

A `ContentProvider` is a mechanism in Android for exchanging content and provide it to different applications.

ContentProviders use URIs starting with *content://* that point to resources accessible through ContentProviders. They read information from sources such as SQLite databases or big files, and they need to be declared in the *AndroidManifest.xml* to be fully functional.

Each application can define its own `ContentProvider`, and Android also provides a comprehensive list of default ContentProviders. This list includes, but is not limited to, access to contacts, SMS, phone numbers and photographs.

QUESTION 11: WHAT IS A BROADCASTRECEIVER?

A `BroadCastReceiver` is a component that delivers a message system-wide, so any other component can capture it and interact with it. There are many of them provided from Android OS, such as broadcast to indicate a low level of battery, a disconnection of the WiFi or network or the turning on or off of a of a screen. However, custom BroadcastReceivers can also be defined in an application (and also declared in the *AndroidManifest.xml*)

QUESTION 12: WHAT IS ADB? MENTION AT LEAST THREE OPERATIONS YOU CAN PERFORM WITH ADB

ADB stands for Android Debug Bridge, and is a command line tool developed to communicate with Android devices, whether they are emulators or physical devices. There are many different operations we can perform with ADB:

-Install or uninstall an application from the device

-Push or pull a file into or from the device

-Access the Logcat of the device.

QUESTION 13: WHAT IS THE DDMS, AND WHAT CAN YOU DO WITH IT?

DDMS stands for Dalvik Debug Monitor Server. It is a tool used for debugging that can perform multiple actions:

- It provides the possibility to capture screenshots from the device.
- There is an analyzer of active Threads and of the Heap state, very helpful in dealing with memory issues and leaks.
- It can simulate locations, incoming SMSes or incoming calls, and deals with Activity recreation.
- There is an integrated file explorer.

The DDMS can be opened with the ddms command from the terminal.

QUESTION 14: WHAT IS AN ASYNCTASK IN ANDROID? IS IT POSSIBLE TO USE IT TO UPDATE THE UI? CAN YOU DEFINE ITS STRUCTURE?

An AsyncTask is a class used to perform short background operations. It can be used to publish results on the UI Thread (for example, after reading data from a

WebService).

`AsyncTask` has four important methods that can be overridden to customize its behavior:

-`onPreExecute()`: Prior to the execution of the `AsyncTask`, this method is called and variables that are taking part in the execution of the `AsyncTask` (for example, a network client) can be initialized.

-`doInBackground()`: when the method start() of the `AsyncTask` is called, the method `doInBackbround()` gets called. This method defines the actual operation that takes place.

-`onProgressUpdate()`: anytime the `AsyncTask` is operating, this method is called. A classical usage of this function is to update a `ProgressBar` to show that there is some progress taking place during the operation.

-`onPostExecute()` This method is called after the `AsyncTask` has performed its task. Here we can close open connections or update the UI with the desired results.

> `AsyncTask` has changed from running serially to running parallel in different Android versions. A candidate being able to recall this and its implications get extra points

QUESTION 15: WHAT IS A PNG9 IMAGE? HOW ARE THEY DIFFERENT FROM NORMAL PNG FILES?

A PNG9 file is a special PNG format that can resize by itself and adapt automatically to different screen sizes. This is something particularly handy when it comes to Android development, since there is a huge fragmentation and is virtually impossible to create a universal application to cover every device.

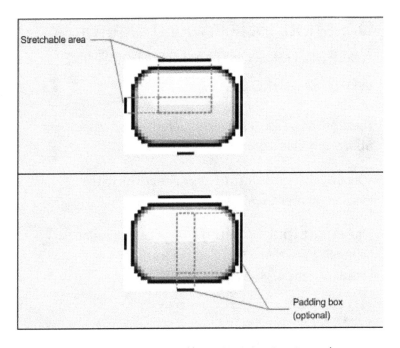

Image obtained from http://developer.android.com/

PNG9 files contain an extra pixel in each side of the image. The left and upper sides indicate the area that will be stretched depending on the size of the screen. The right and down sides indicate the padding that will be left between the borders and the content, again depending on the size of the target screen.

QUESTION 16: IF I WOULD LIKE TO ACCESS THE POSITION OF MY DEVICE, WHAT SHOULD I DO?

There are a few classes involved in retrieving the location from an Android device.

-The `LocationManager` provides access to the location services from the Android system.

-The `LocationListener` allows the application to be notified whether a Provider, the Status or the Location of the device has changed.

QUESTION 17: WHAT IS A FRAMELAYOUT? CAN YOU THINK OF WHEN TO USE IT?

A `FrameLayout` is a special type of view in Android that is used to block an area of the screen, in order to display a single element (very often used to display and position Fragments on the screen). It can however also accept multiple children.

The items added to the `FrameLayout` are put in a stack, with the most recently added element at the top. If there are several children, the dimension of the

`FrameLayout` will be the dimension of its bigger child (plus any padding if it was originally added to the `FrameLayout`).

QUESTION 18: WHAT IS A VIEW IN ANDROID?

A `View` in Android is the most basic element to build a UI element. A View is contained in the package *android.view.view*. Views occupy a rectangular area on the screen, and they capture interaction events with the view. They also render on the screen the content anytime it has been updated.

QUESTION 19: CAN YOU CREATE CUSTOM VIEWS? HOW?

To extend an Android `View` and create our own one, we need to create a class that inherits from the View class, and that has at least a constructor that receives an object `Context` and another one `AttributeSet`, as follows:

```
class ExampleView extends View {
    public ExampleView (Context context,
AttributeSet attrs) {
        super(context, attrs);
    }
```

}

If you want to create custom attributes for a custom View, you need to declare a *<declare-styleable>* resource element, and add it the custom attributes you need.

QUESTION 20: WHAT ARE VIEWGROUPS AND THEIR DIFFERENCE FROM VIEWS?

A ViewGroup extends from the View class. A ViewGroup is the base class used to create Layouts, which are containers for different sets of Views (or other ViewGroups).

QUESTION 21: EXPLAIN THE MOST RELEVANT ATTRIBUTES FROM VIEWS YOU CAN THINK OF.

We can explain a few key attributes here:

-*layout_width* and *height*. The possible value can be **FILL_PARENT**, **MATCH_PARENT** or **WRAP_CONTENT**.

-Gravity: The gravity indicates the positioning of an item within a larger container.

ID. Is one of the most important attributes in an Android

View. It is used later for accessing the view and refer to it.

> A more experimented developer should be able to answer "what problems can we have in an Android application if the views are not being recreated after a screen rotation?" The answer is that Android looks for IDs of each element, and an item not having an ID will therefore not be found and not recreated

QUESTION 22: WHAT IS A LAYOUT IN ANDROID?

A Layout in Android is a representation of a UI component, contained in items such as Fragments or Widgets. A Layout can either be contained in an XML file, or it can be instantiated at runtime (View and ViewGroup can be created and manipulated programmatically.

QUESTION 23: CAN YOU NAME A FEW LAYOUT TYPES FOR ANDROID?

There are a few common types of `Layout`:

–`LinearLayout`: it arranges all the elements on a single row, displayed either horizontally or vertically. By default the orientation is horizontal.

–`RelativeLayout`: in this layout all the elements can be displayed in relation to other elements or to their parents.

-A `TableLayout` displays elements as in a traditional table, with rows and columns. It extends from `LinearLayout`.

-Grid View: similar to the `TableLayout`. Items are displayed in a bi-dimensional grid that can have any possible dimensions.

QUESTION 24: WHAT IS THE SUPPORT LIBRARY, AND WHY WAS INTRODUCED?

To deal with the Fragmentation among different versions of Android, the Support Library was introduced first in 2011. The support library package contains a set of libraries to provide backwards compatibility with previous versions of Android (for instance, to use Fragments in versions of Android previous to the 3.x).

QUESTION 25: WHAT IS THE FRAGMENTATION IN ANDROID? DO YOU KNOW ANY TECHNIQUES YOU CAN USE TO AVOID IT?

The fragmentation in Android happens due to the large number of OS versions and different devices using Android OS – the problem does not happen on other mobile platforms that have a unique hardware manufacturer, such as iOS. Fragmentation is a threat to the ability of running a single Android APK created with the standard Android SDK through the entire Android ecosystem, since there will be many versions not supporting all the features.

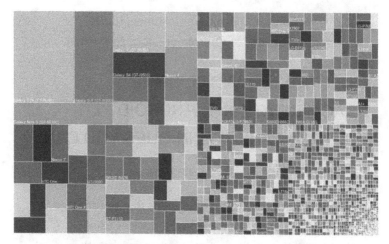

Image obtained from http://www.macerkopf.de

Each of these squares represent a different device, and their size is proportional to the amount of devices.

There is no silver bullet to prevent fragmentation from happening, but there are some basic measures we can apply to make our application work on most devices.

-Use resources for each resolution. Do not just create default resources: create one for each resolution type.

-Use the elements from the Android Compatibility Library as much as possible, so they can run on all Android versions.

-Avoid absolute positioning. You should always aim for relative positioning of your Layouts.

QUESTION 26: WHAT IS THE RESOURCE FOLDER, AND WHAT IS IT USED FOR?

Resources are additional content (such as images or strings) that are packed and delivered with the application. An application can access and use these files in its own context.

There are different types of folders, each includes different type of resources. The resources are typically packed in XML, image formats, etc.

-**animator**: files defining animations

-**color**: folder defining a list of colors.

-**drawable**: Bitmap files or XML defining images for different states.

- **layout**: folder defining layout files

-**raw**: this folder is used to include arbitrary files that cannot be classified in the other categories.

-**values**: different type of values are included within this folder (strings, integers, arrays, etc).

Question 27: Can you mention some of the characteristics of the OO programming languages?

The Object Oriented Programming (OO) is a modeling paradigm to build software that is more modular, easier to maintain and more flexible. It has the following main features.

-Encapsulation: OO provide objects the ability to encapsulate their internal behavior and attributes into classes. The attributes are hidden, and their state can only be modified through the use of accessor functions. This increases modularity and maintenance of the code, since objects cannot interact among themselves in an undesired way.

-Polymorphism: is the ability of the OO to present the same adaptable interface to different data types. A polymorphic function or type will be adaptable based on the data type that is requesting it.

-Inheritance: this is the basis of reusing code. Using inheritance we can create relationships between objects that extend from parent objects, and inherit their behavior and internal structure.

-Abstraction: abstracting an object means to separate the idea of an object from the implementation details.

QUESTION 28: WHAT IS THE DIFFERENCE BETWEEN OVERRIDING AND OVERLOADING A METHOD IN JAVA?

Overriding a method removes its original behavior, and let a new behavior to be rewritten (we can however called the behavior of the parent method with `super.methodName()` and re-use it if required.

Overloading a method happens when the name for two different methods is the same, but the parameters are different.

QUESTION 29: WHAT IS THE DIFFERENT BETWEEN AN INTERFACE AND AN ABSTRACT CLASS?

An interface is absolutely abstracted, and cannot be implemented. It defines the behavior that a object will need to perform, without providing any details about it.

An abstract class cannot be instantiated, but it can partially or totally define behavior and internal structure for an object.

Interfaces are always implemented, and objects always do extend from abstract classes.

QUESTION 30: WHAT DOES THE STATIC WORD MEAN IN JAVA?

In general terms, the word static means that a member of a class can be accessed without instantiating an object of its class.

> Is it possible to override static methods in Java? The answer is no, because overriding is based on dynamic binding at runtime, and static members are being bound during compilation time.

QUESTION 31: WHAT DOES IT MEAN WHEN AN OBJECT IS PASSED BY REFERENCE OR BY VALUE?

When an object is being passed to a function by value, a copy of the object is passed and the original object is never modified. The opposite applies to an object passed as a reference: the object itself is sent to the function being directly modified.

An object in Java is always passed by value.

QUESTION 32: WHY IS THE USAGE OF HASHCODE() AND EQUALS() IMPORTANT IN JAVA?

The usage of hashCode() and equals() is crucial when we start using HashMaps. A HashMap uses both functions to determine the index of keys and to detect duplicates. By implementing those methods in the target classes, the efficiency and accuracy of the HashMap increases.

QUESTION 33: WHAT DOES THE INTERFACE SERIALIZABLE DO IN JAVA?

Serialization is the process of translating an object into binary information so it can be stored in a database or be sent through a network request without losing information. To make an object Serializable in Java, we need to implement the interface **java.io.Serializable**

Chapter 2. That guy who has already been working with Android for some time.

The following chapter includes questions that are aimed for very experienced developers, typically with 1-2 or 3 years of experience. They feels comfortable and familiar with the SDK and most of the libraries used for Android development. They have probably been working on their own framework or architecture for Android development, and can identify complex problems and provide solutions for them.

Question 34: what is Dependency Injection? Do you use any DI library in your project? Can you name a few of them, and why one is better than others?

Dependency Injection is a design pattern to implement inversion of control, and to resolve dependencies. Dependency Injection (DI) eliminates boilerplate code (for example, by removing listener) and provides a much cleaner and effective code.

There are a few DI libraries used in Android development:

-Dagger[5]

-ButterKnife[6]

-RoboGuice[7]

ButterKnife and Dagger do not use reflection, but rather compile time annotations. They are therefore faster to develop with.

QUESTION 35: WHICH CLASSES CAN YOU USE FOR THREADING IN ANDROID?

Android provide several different classes to handle threading:

−AsyncTask: One of the first classes introduced in Android since 1.6. It encapsulates a background process, that synchronizes with the main thread.

−Handler: a Handler object can send Messages and Runnable objects. Each Handler is always associated with a different Thread.

---

[5] http://square.github.io/dagger/
[6] http://jakewharton.github.io/butterknife/
[7] https://github.com/roboguice/roboguice

-Threads: this is the default Java class for Threads. It extends from **java.util.concurrent**. It is somewhat antiquated, and there is some functionality lacking for modern software environments (i.e., no default pooling or handling configuration changes)

QUESTION 36: WHAT IS ORM? DO YOU KNOW AND USE AN ORM LIBRARY IN ANDROID? WHAT ARE THEIR ADVANTAGES AND DISADVANTAGES?

ORM stands for Object-Relational mapping. Is a technique to match objects definition and storage options, typically databases.

Android does not provide it natively, but there are a few frameworks available:

-SugarORM[8]

-GreenDAO[9]

-ORMLite[10]

-ActiveAndroid[11]

---

[8] http://satyan.github.io/sugar/
[9] http://greendao-orm.com/
[10] http://ormlite.com/
[11] http://www.activeandroid.com/

-Realm[12]

Each library has different features, and we might want to decide on using one or the other depending on our requirements. GreenDao is a lightweight (>100kb), fast library designed specifically for Android. Nearly all the present libraries use reflection, which is generally a worse alternative than annotations processing. SugarORM simplifies CRUD by only using three methods. ORMLite is a Java library, therefore being less light than other alternatives and providing more functionality.

QUESTION 37: WHAT IS A LOADER?

`Loader` and `LoaderManager` classes were introduced in Android 3.0 in an attempt to remove workload from the main thread. A `Loader` performs an asynchronous loading of data in an `Activity` or a `Fragment`. They are continuously monitoring the source of their data, and when it changes they deliver the new data.

QUESTION 38: WHAT ARE SOFT AND WEAK REFERENCES IN JAVA?

A strong reference that is not eligible for garbage collection, and they are our regular object references.

---

[12] https://realm.io/

```
MyObject object = new MyObject();
```

If an object is always reachable through a series of strong references, it can never get collected. This is what we normally want, but we might want to force a collection.

A weak reference is not binding an object into memory. An object weakly referenced will be collected in the next execution of the garbage collector. Java provides some default collections that use weak objects, such as `WeakHashMap`.

> There are also Phantom and Soft references. They are less known, but are also useful in many contexts.
>
> A developer able to recognize them and explain what they are used for has more than the average knowledge of memory management in Java.

QUESTION 39: WHAT IS AIDL IN ANDROID?

Android implement some *Interprocess Communication Mechanisms* (IPC) to communicate between different applications. Some basic ones are the `Intent` or the

`ContentProvider.`

AIDL stands for **Android Interface Definition Language**, and it allows a developer to create an interface for a server and a client application to communicate. This is a more complex solution than for example the Intents, and increases the possibilities of communication between processes.

QUESTION 40: HOW CAN YOU ENSURE THE CONFIDENTIALITY OF YOUR CODE IN ANDROID?

There are several security measures we can take to make our code more difficult to reverse by an attacker, but the main answer is to use ProGuard[13]. ProGuard is a Java obfuscator provided in most of the Android environments, which Increases security in our code by performing different obfuscation techniques in our code.

---

[13] http://proguard.sourceforge.net/

Ask about problems or limitations of ProGuard:

-Strings are not obfuscated

-ProGuard needs to exclude many libraries from our code to ensure that the code is running smoothly and free of problems

-ProGuard can be used in combination with the NDK to increase the protection level of our code

QUESTION 41: WHAT IS THE NDK, AND WHY IS IT USEFUL?

NDK (Native Development Kit) allows a developer to reuse C/C++ code into our native application. It makes performance better, and we can make use of many of the already available libraries, such as OpenCV[14].

---

[14] http://opencv.org/platforms/android.html

QUESTION 42: WHAT IS AN ANR? WHICH STRATEGIES CAN YOU USE TO AVOID IT?

ANR stands for Application Not Responding, and is a dialog that pops up during execution time when an application cannot respond to user input

This generally happens because there is work being performed on the UI Thread that is either blocked, waiting for a response or performing intensive computation.

There is a set of strategies we can use to avoid the ANR screen:

-Perform methods that might block the screen in an `AsyncTask` and inside the method `doInBackground()`. The UI will keep running regardless of the method behavior.

-Reinforce responsiveness: Google points out that 100ms to 200ms is the threshold beyond which users will realize that the application is slowing down. If such period is expected to happen, provide some visual feedback to the user (such a `ProgressDialog`) to let them know there is a background operation taking place.

-Use `StrictMode` to identify performance bottlenecks and access to the Main Thread.

QUESTION 43: WHAT IS THE STRICTMODE?

The `StrictMode` is a developer tool that can be enabled, and that will identify all the access to the Main Thread from any process that is not supposed to be doing it (such as network or database access). The `StrictMode` is typically only activated during development, and it should not affect an application in production.

QUESTION 44: CAN YOU MENTION SOME TYPES OF TESTING YOU KNOW?

An Android application can typically run different tests:

-UI Tests: they involve user interaction, and verify that an app is behaving correctly in different scenarios with different data.

-Unit Test: Unitary test are based on the JUnit framework, and they can test the output of any class, check that a manager is correctly handling a set of mocked data, and that it is producing the right output.

-Integration Test: they verify that the integration and collaboration between different modules is effective and working.

QUESTION 45: DO YOU SEE A DIFFERENCE BETWEEN FLAVORS AND PROJECT LIBRARIES? HOW WOULD THEY APPLY IN DIFFERENT SITUATIONS?

Product Flavors are used when a single project must return different versions of the same application. Think for instance of an application that needs to use GoogleMaps vs. another application that needs to use Blackberry or Bing Maps. Or a free vs. a paid application.

A library is a packaging of common functionality that will be reused in different applications and eventually to third party members that will require making use of it.

As the Gradle Plugin User Guide states, "if the answer to "Is this the same application?" is yes, then this [product flavor] is probably the way to go over Library Projects."

QUESTION 46: WHAT IS THE BUILDTYPE IN GRADLE? WHAT CAN YOU USE IT FOR?

Gradle defines a type called BuildType. This means the application can be built in different configurations. By default we do it in debug and release, but many more can be added manually.

A BuildType is added as follows:

```
buildTypes {
    newBuildType {
    }
}
```

In the BuildType we can define variables and access them later from a java file. This is very handy if, for example, you have different servers that deliver different information based on the build type. In that case you might want to retrieve the value BuildType.SERVER_NAME. You can also use it define different types of Tokens (Google Analytic is a good example, since you do not want a debug version to interfere with the data of the Production version).

QUESTION 47: WHAT IS THE DIFFERENCE BETWEEN SERIALIZABLE AND PARCELABLE, AND WHICH ALTERNATIVE IS BETTER TO USE IN ANDROID?

`Parcelable` is a class that has been specifically designed for Android, and is thus more efficient than `Serializable`.

`Serializable` just needs an interface to be implemented, thus being more comfortable for the developer. It does however use reflection, and it is a slow process. It also creates a few temporary objects and there are some concerns with the garbage collector.

`Parcelable` generates, however, boilerplate code. Most of the time we will prefer it over `Serializable`, but performance will come at a cost.

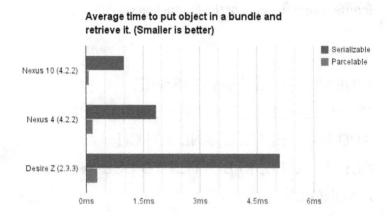

Average time to put object in a bundle and retrieve it. (Smaller is better)

QUESTION 48: WHAT IS REFLECTION?

Reflection refers to code that is able to inspect itself or some other code in the system.

In static typing system language such as Java, we cannot call a method whose name we know, unless we also know the interface it conforms to.

```
Method method =
foo.getClass().getMethod("doSomething",
null); method.invoke(foo, null);
```

Abusing reflection can have an impact in terms of performance and stability, since classes need to be semantically analyzed and an object might expect a component in a class that might not exist.

QUESTION 49: DO YOU HAVE EXPERIENCE WITH LINT? WHAT IS IT USED FOR?

Lint is a tool that scans the code statically and can provide a report with potential bugs, issues with the code style and tips about optimization and performance.

Lint is integrated in IDEs such as Android Studio, but it can also be run from the command line or integrated in a Continuous Integration server.

QUESTION 50: WHAT IS A SURFACEVIEW?

A `SurfaceView` is a custom view in Android that can be used to draw inside it.

The main difference between a View and a `SurfaceView` is that a View is drawn in the UI Thread, which is used for all the user interaction.

If you want to update the UI rapidly enough and render a good amount of information in it, a `SurfaceView` is a better choice.

There are a few technical insides to the `SurfaceView` that an experienced developer would like to mention

-They are not hardware accelerated.

-Normal views are rendered when the methods invalidate() or `postInvalidate()` are called, but this does not mean the view will be immediately updated (A VSYNC will be sent, and the OS decides when it gets updated. The `SurfaceView` can be immediately updated.

-A `SurfaceView` has an allocated surface buffer, so it is more costly

QUESTION 51: HOW WOULD YOU IMPLEMENT A LIST IN ANDROID, USING A LISTVIEW OR A RECYCLERVIEW?

Google created `RecyclerView` as an improvement over `ListView`. You can still use a `ListView`, but `RecyclerView` brings several advantages.

-You can reuse cells while you are scrolling

-The list can be decoupled from the container

-`RecyclerView` can easily accept any type of content within its cell without much trouble.

QUESTION 52: IS THERE ANYWAY TO IMPLEMENT PUSH NOTIFICATIONS IN ANDROID?

Android natively supports push notifications with the Cloud Messaging[15] (formerly Android Cloud to Device Framework).

QUESTION 53: CAN YOU THINK OF HOW TWO FRAGMENTS CAN COMMUNICATE?

There are many different ways in which two different fragments in Android can communicate, but a very useful one could be the following.

---

[15] https://developers.google.com/cloud-messaging/

Suppose we have an `Activity` that is hosting two different Fragments, and the `Fragment` A wants to send some information to the `Fragment` B.

Our Activity will implement an interface defined in the Fragment A that defines a method "`sendInformation()`". The interface can be called in the `Fragment` A, and the `Activity` will receive the event. Then the Activity will implement in the method "`sendInformation()`" how the second `Fragment` will handle this information.

> This is a very open discussion and there are a lot of possible answers. A more experienced developer could talk about Event Driven Programming or Reactive Programming

QUESTION 54: IN AN INSTRUMENTATION TESTCASE, WHAT ARE THE TWO MOST IMPORTANT METHODS?

An Android Intrumentation Test implements two very important methods

```
protected void setUp()
protected void tearDown()
```

setUp() runs the testing environment is initialized.
tearDown() runs immediately after the test to close
connections or restore the status of the testing
environment.

BONUS:

The setUp() functions is always called before each
individual test is passed. A confident developer will know
that if we run two different tests, this will be the
execution flow:

```
constructor()
setUp();
testXXX();
tearDown();

setUp();
testXXX2();
tearDown();
```

QUESTION 55: HOW DOES ANDROID KNOW THAT A FUNCTION IN A FILE IS A TEST THAT NEEDS TO BE RUN?

Using reflection. Android looks inside a test file for all the
functions that start with the prefix "test", and runs them.

If you try with a function called `pleaseRunThisFunction()` it will not run.

QUESTION 56: BY DEFAULT, IN WHICH THREAD WILL A SERVICE RUN WHEN DECLARED IN THE ANDROIDMANIFEST?

A `Service` will always run in the `Thread` of its hosting process. Therefore, if a user is performing costly operations in a `Service` started from an `Activity`, it will likely block it and display an ANR.

For this situation there are better alternatives, such as an `AsyncTask`.

QUESTION 57: IS A CONTEXT ALWAYS REFERING AN ACTIVITY OR AN APPLICATION?

No. A `Context` can provide access to many different types (`Application`, `Activity`, `Service`, `BroadcastReceiver`, `ContentProvider`). Depending on the element that is being sent as a `Context`, we will be able to perform different actions (such as starting an `Activity` or showing a `Dialog`).

QUESTION 58: WHAT IS A PENDINGINTENT?

A `PendingIntent` is similar to an `Intent`. It is given to foreign or third party application and provides them with permission to execute a particular piece of code in an application. It is used very often with classes such as `NotificationManager`, `AlarmManager` or `AppWidgetManager`.

QUESTION 59: CAN YOU PROVIDE SOME IDEAS ON HOW TO PREVENT MEMORY LEAKS IN YOUR APP?

There are many strategies that can be applied. Here are just a small set of ideas.

-It is better to use an `Application Context` rather than an `Activity Context`, since `Activities` are more likely to be leaked.

-It is generally good to avoid having long-lived references to Activities.

-It is better to avoid non-static inner classes in Activities unless we control their lifecycle. It is better to use static inner classes with weak references, so they can't be collected when they are not used.

There is a library published by
Square called Leak Canary[16]. A
candidate with knowledge about
this library will likely have
experience fixing memory leaks

QUESTION 60: CAN AN APPLICATION START ON REBOOT OR WHEN THE DEVICE IS BEING STARTED?

This question is important, since for many in-house applications the purpose will be to block the device and allow only operating with one application.

Making usage of a `BroadcastReceiver` with an `Intent` Filter, as follows, can do this.

```
<receiver android-
permission="android.permission.RECEIVE_BOO
T_COMPLETED" android:name="YourReceiver" >
    <intent-filter >
    <action

android:name="android.intent.action.SCREEN
_ON" />
<action
android:name="android.intent.action.BOOT_C
OMPLETED" />
```

---

[16] https://github.com/square/leakcanary

```
</intent-filter>
</receiver>
```

QUESTION 61: WOULD YOU UPDATE AN ITEM IN YOUR SCREEN PERIODICALLY WITH A TIMERTASK OR A HANDLER? WHY?

With a `Handler`, which is the way to do it in Android. Using a `TimerTask` introduces a new `Thread` for a relatively small reason.

QUESTION 62: WHAT DOES THE KEYWORD SYNCHRONIZED MEAN IN JAVA?

As quoted from Sun: Synchronized methods enable a simple strategy for preventing thread interference and memory consistency errors: if an object is visible to more than one thread, all reads or writes to that object's variables are done through synchronized methods.

This is a non trivial field in Java, but basically helps that when two threads are accessing the same resources, this is done atomically and prevent incorrect accesses and deadlocks.

QUESTION 63: HOW CAN YOU MANUALLY START THE GARBAGE COLLECTOR?

A call to `System.gc()` tells the system that the Garbage Collector is required and should be started. There is no guarantee, however, that the GC will start running immediately. It is up to the JVM to start it sooner or later based on the system priorities, memory and processor status.

QUESTION 64: WHAT IS THE DIFFERENCE BETWEEN INTEGER AND INT?

Integer is a class defined in **java.lang**, whereas int is a primitive type from Java and a Java keyword. When you need to use a function that requires to be passed an Object, you can send an object of the type Integer as a parameter wrapping a value of type int. Same applies for all the wrapper types (Float, etc).

QUESTION 65: HOW DOES INTEGER.PARSEINT(STRING) WORK?

The purpose of this type of questions is not to know that an engineer remembers piece by piece the entire code that performs `parseInt()` - who does, I have never seen the current code! -but to put him on thinking.

Integer is a wrapper class around int. While a string cannot be translated directly into string, we can (character by character) access it and convert it into an integer.

This is an approximate version of what a candidate should answer.

> - init some result with the value 0
> - for each character in the string
>   parameter do
>   - ○ result = result * 10
>   - ○ get the digit from the character
>   - ○ add the digit to the result
> - return result

QUESTION 66: CAN YOU MENTION A PATTERN YOU REGULARLY USE WHILE PROGRAMMING, AND EXPLAIN HOW IT WORKS?

There are hundreds of available patterns and entire books dedicated to them, and it will be very sumptuous to think we could explain them better in this book. However, the right candidate should feel comfortable taking 2 or 3 patterns he uses frequently and explain

them. As a small set of suggestions, I deal almost daily
with the following patterns in my code.

-MVC

-Observer

-Iterator

-Singleton

-Builder

CHAPTER 3. WE NEED THAT GUY ON BOARD, WE WANT TO DO GREAT THINGS!

The following chapter is dedicated to the upper level of the Android engineers, those with several years of experience and have typically worked in a broad variety of projects with a bigger variety of requirements.

Remember that experience needs to be combined with analytical and solving skills, and you do not want to hire for your organization a candidate that just reads this book and memorize it by heart. Especially in this chapter, you want to engage in discussions and opinion exchange. Sometimes there is single solution to real time problems, and in most of the cases solutions involve a trade-off: you will need to give up in performance to achieve code usability, etc.

Senior Developers also require leadership and motivational skills to lead a team. This book does not cover possible questions and tricks to identify those skills, but I am sure the hypothetical reader has already some clues on how to identify them. Senior Developers must be comfortable and self-confident while discussing any topic, and open to embrace change and difference. They create an entrepreneur atmosphere around them; they are servant leaders rather than bosses and encourage independence and freethinking.

QUESTION 67: WHAT ARE TRANSIENT AND VOLATILE MODIFIERS?

`volatile` and `transient` modifiers can be applied to fields in classes.

A `transient` modifier prevents a variable from being serialized. When the object is deserialized, is then initialized to the default value (null for a reference type, 0 or false for a primitive type).

A `volatile` field can be accessed by other threads, so the compiler allows access to them.

QUESTION 68: WHY ARE TRANSIENT AND VOLATILE USEFUL IN THE CONTEXT OF A PROGRAM? CAN YOU PROVIDE AN EXAMPLE?

When fields in a class are derived from other fields, we very likely want to prevent them from being serialized, so they can be recreated again from the original field.

```
class GalleryImage implements Serializable {
```

```java
    private Image image;
    private transient Image thumbnailImage;

    private void generateThumbnail()      {}

    private void readObject(ObjectInputStream
        inputStream) throws IOException,
ClassNotFoundException      {
        inputStream.defaultReadObject();
        generateThumbnail();
    }
}
```

In this example, the thumbnailImage is generated from the originalImage field. When an object of the type GalleryImage is deserialized, we would like to recreate thumbnailImage rather than deserializing it.

volatile can be useful, for example, to stop threads. A common example is to declare a boolean flag in a thread. If we can to access and stop this thread from another one, the thread can set the flag to true and stop the thread if required.

```java
public class Foo extends Thread {

    private volatile boolean close = false;

    public void run() {
        while(!close) {
            // do work
        }
```

```
        }

    public void close() {
        close = true;
        // interrupt here if needed
    }
}
```

Note that there is no need to use synchronized
here.

QUESTION 69: CAN YOU WRITE SOME CODE THAT CAUSES A JAVA MEMORY LEAK?

For example, a connection that is not closed

```
try {
    Connection conn =
ConnectionFactory.getConnection();
    ...
    ... } catch (Exception e) {
        e.printStacktrace();
        }
```

An open stream

```
try {
    BufferedReader br = new
BufferedReader(new FileReader(inputFile));
    ...
    ...
```

```
} catch (Exception e) {
    e.printStacktrace();
}
```

Or a static final field holding a reference to an object

```
class MemorableClass {
    static final ArrayList list = new
ArrayList(100);
}
```

QUESTION 70: COULD YOU DESCRIBE WHAT EACH TYPE OF CONTEXT CAN DO? FOR EXAMPLE, CAN I START AN ACTIVITY USING AN APPLICATION CONTEXT?

Dave Smith, from Double Encore, wrote the following table in one of his blog posts. A Senior candidate should feel comfortable reasoning it. Please note that nobody should know this table by heart, but being able to deduce it.

	Application	Activity	Service	ContentProvider	BroadcastReceiver
Show a Dialog	NO	YES	NO	NO	NO

	Application	Activity	Service	ContentProvider	BroadcastReceiver
Start an Activity	NO[1]	YES	NO[1]	NO[1]	NO[1]
Layout Inflation	NO[2]	YES	NO[2]	NO[2]	NO[2]
Start a Service	YES	YES	YES	YES	YES
Bind to a Service	YES	YES	YES	YES	NO
Send a Broadcast	YES	YES	YES	YES	YES
Register BroadcastReceiver	YES	YES	YES	YES	NO[3]
Load Resource Values	YES	YES	YES	YES	YES

QUESTION 71: WHICH OF THE FOLLOWING METHODS IS BETTER TO USE IN ANDROID?

```java
public void zero() {
    int sum = 0;
    for (int i = 0; i < mArray.length; ++i) {
        sum += mArray[i].mSplat;
    }
}

public void one() {
    int sum = 0;
    Foo[] localArray = mArray;
    int len = localArray.length;

    for (int i = 0; i < len; ++i) {
        sum += localArray[i].mSplat;
    }
}

public void two() {
    int sum = 0;
    for (Foo a : mArray) {
        sum += a.mSplat;
    }

}
```

The method two() is the fastest of all of them. In

`zero()` JIT cannot optimize the cost that mans retrieving the length of the array everytime. In `one()` everything is pulled out into local variables. `two()` will be faster in devices without a JIT, and same speed as `one()` in devices with a JIT.

QUESTION 72: CAN YOU THINK OF A LIMITATION OF PROGUARD, AND WHICH OTHER PRODUCT CAN OVERCOME IT?

ProGuard does not obfuscate strings from an application, so they are always visible after applying it.

We can think of two immediate solutions: using NDK we can store the strings in a natively compiled file and access it through JNI, although this is security by obscurity and it can be criticized. The other method is to use an engine such as DexGuard[17], which also obfuscates Strings.

17

https://www.guardsquare.com/software/dexguard-enterprise

QUESTION 73: WHAT ARE THE DIFFERENCES BETWEEN DALVIK AND ART?

Dalvik and ART are different machines and they operate differently. The most important difference to the developer is that ART operates much faster. The DEX bytecode is translated into machine code during installation, so no extra time is needed to compile it (Dalvik uses Just-In-Time compilation, whereas ART uses Ahead-Of-Time compilation)

Dalvik requires extra memory for the JIT Cache, so it also requires more space for the app. These factors combined means that ART in general improves the battery life.

QUESTION 74: DO YOU KNOW TOOLS YOU CAN USE TO ACCESS THE SOURCE CODE OF AN APPLICATION?

Even if the source code of an application has been obfuscated with ProGuard, there is a free set of tools available that we can use to reverse engineer an application and access its source code.

-ApkTool [18]disassembles a file very nearly to its original

---

[18] http://ibotpeaches.github.io/Apktool/

form.

-Dex2Jar[19] translates .dex files into .class files. Therefore it is easy to read with some other application.

-Java Decompiler [20] can open jar files and present them in the form of Java files (so it can read for examples the files that have been translated with Dex2Jar.

QUESTION 75: WHAT DOES CLASS.FORNAME METHOD DO?

A call to `Class.forName("x")` loads the class X dynamically at runtime. If the class X is not found, the compiler will return a `ClassNotFoundException`.

QUESTION 76: HOW CAN YOU OPTIMIZE VIEW USAGE IN AN ANDROID APPLICATION?

There are different answers to this question:

-Using the <merge> tag, which will reduce the number of level in view trees.

---

[19] https://github.com/pxb1988/dex2jar
[20] http://jd.benow.ca/

-Using ViewStub. A ViewStub is a lightweight view with no dimension that does not draw anything and does not participate in any action of the layout. They are therefore cheap to inflate. A Layout that has been referenced by a ViewStub is only inflated when you decide to.

-Reusing layouts with <include>

QUESTION 77: THERE ARE TWO BIG LIBRARIES USED FOR ANDROID TESTING, ESPRESSO AND ROBOTIUM. CAN YOU MENTION ONE BIG ADVANTAGE OF ESPRESSO OVER ROBOTIUM?

The major one is that Espresso is synchronized, whether Robotium is not. That means that many times a test developed with Robotium will just fail because the UI has not been updated but the test is expecting to perform a click or interact with the user screen.

A better error reporting and a clearer API are reasons that some people might not agree with Espresso's superiority but the synchronization is a objective major advantage.

QUESTION 78: WHAT IS THE PERMGEN IN JAVA?

PermGen is the place where the VM in Java stores all the metadata information about the classes in the application. Generally the JVM manages automatically the PermGen and it does not require any further tuning, although memory leaks can happen if there is a problem loading the classes.

> PerGerm does not exist anymore since Java 8, having been replaced by metaspace. Java 8 is generally not possible to use for Android development, but a candidate being able to point this facts shows a wide understanding of the memory management in Java

QUESTION 79: DO YOU KNOW THE FUNCTION ONTRIMMEMORY()?

This is a callback called when the OS decides that is a good moment to optimize memory from the running processes. For example, when an Activity goes in the background and there is no enough memory to keep alive all the running processes. There are different level for `onTrimMemory`, and these can be retrieved with `ActivityManager.getMyMemoryState(RunningAppProcessInfo)`.

QUESTION 80: IS IT POSSIBLE TO RUN AN ANDROID APP IN MULTIPLE PROCESSES?

Yes. By default, an application runs in a process. Android devices can only support 24/36/48 MB for a single process (and even less in smaller devices). When we start an Android application, a process is forked from Zygote, spawns the main thread and run the main Activity. We can however run different processes by using **android:process**. For example, the following lines will make the service RenderVideogame to be run on a different process.

```
<service
    android:name=".RenderVideogame "
    android:process=":renderVideogame"
/>
```

QUESTION 81: CAN YOU SAY SOMETHING IN TERMS OF PERFORMANCE ABOUT USING INT, FLOAT AND DOUBLE?

As a rule of thumb, a float variable is twice as slower as an int. float and double are the same in terms of speed, but double needs twice as much space as a float variable.

QUESTION 82: HOW WOULD YOU OPTIMIZE THE SCROLLING OF A LISTVIEW THAT HAS BEEN LOADED WITH HEAVY ELEMENTS?

There are a few options that can be used to make the scrolling of a ListView lighter.

-Using a ViewHolder pattern: using an object ViewHolder can prevent the system to call continuously the function findViewById(), therefore preventing the scrolling to be slowed down.

-Using a Background Thread. If you make use of heavy components (for example, images) use an AsyncTask to load them dynamically on the list rather than load them statically.

QUESTION 83: WHAT IS SMP? WHAT RELATIONSHIP DOES IT HAVE WITH ANDROID?

SMP stands for Symmetric Multi-Processor. It describes an architecture for multiple processors accessing memory.

Android was supporting a unique processor architecture until Android 3.0. Most of the Android devices have different cores, so it makes sense to make use of them (even if they are natively prepared to run applications only in one processor, and use the other ones for secondary tasks). Android provides a set of do and don'ts, such as not abusing volatile or synchronized variables.

QUESTION 84: ARE SQL INJECTION ATTACKS VALID IN ANDROID? HOW WOULD YOU PREVENT THEM?

If you are using data and retrieving it from components or network components that at the end perform an SQL query, SQL injections are an issue. Besides using validation in input fields or libraries to avoid SQL injections, another possible solution is to use parameterized queries with ContentProviders, which virtually remove the risk of suffering an SQL Injection.

Question 85: Can you dynamically load code in Android? What this can be used for?

Although not recommended, code can be loaded dynamically from outside the application APK by making use of the class DexClassLoader.

This made sense when there was a limitation to the number of methods an APK could host (65k). Now that Google has solved this, some applications might need to download executable from over the network, but this exposes the security of the system and makes it very vulnerable to tampering or malicious code.

Question 86: What is the Java Heap?

When a program starts, the JVM reserves some memory and uses this memory for all its need and part of this memory is call java heap memory. Heap in Java is generally located at bottom of address space and moves upward. When we want to create objects using the new operator, the object is allocated memory from the Heap and when object dies or is garbage collected, the memory previously used goes back to Heap space in Java.

QUESTION 87: DESCRIBE HOW AN OUTOFMEMORYERROR HAPPENS IN ANDROID

As the application progresses, more objects get created and heap space is expanded to accommodate new objects. The virtual machine runs the garbage collector periodically to reclaim memory back from dead objects. The VM expands the Heap in Java some where near to the maximum heap size, and if there is no more memory left for creating new object in java heap, it will throw a **java.lang.OutOfMemoryError** killing the application. Before throwing OutOfMemoryError the VM tries to run the garbage collector to free any available space but if even after that there is still not much space available on Heap in Java, it will result into an OutOfMemoryError.

QUESTION 88: WHEN WILL BE AN OBJECT BE ELIGIBLE FOR GARBAGE COLLECTION?

When there is no reference alive for that object or if any live thread can't reach it. Garbage collection thread is a daemon thread which will run upon a complex GC algorithm and when it runs it collects all objects which are eligible for GC.

A solid candidate will be able to answer that a cyclic reference doesn't count as a live reference, and if two objects are pointing to each other and there is no live reference for any of them, then both are eligible for GC.

QUESTION 89: WHAT CAN HAPPEN IF A STATIC VARIABLE IS POINTING TO AN ACTIVITY CONTEXT?

Very likely a memory leak when the Activity disappears.

QUESTION 90: WHAT IS A SPANNABLE INTERFACE?

This is the interface for text to which markup objects can be attached and detached. Note that not all Spannable classes have mutable text.

Question 91: How would you upload multiple files to an HTTP server in a single HTTP Request?

Use MIME Multipart. It was thought to send different fragments of information in a single request, and is integrated with most of the native HTTP clients.

Question 92: Does Fragments need a parameterless constructor? Why?

Yes. The instantiate method in the Fragment class calls the newInstance method. Upon instantiation it checks that the accessor is public and that that the class loader allows access to it. This allows the FragmentManager to kill and recreate Fragments with states. (The Android subsystem does similar things with Activities).

Question 93: What is Autoboxing and Unboxing in Java?

Autoboxing is the automatic conversion made by the Java compiler between the primitive types and their corresponding object wrapper classes. For example, the compiler converts an int to an Integer, a double to a Double, and so on. If the conversion goes the other way, this operation is called unboxing.

QUESTION 94: WHAT IS A THREAD POOL?

A Thread pool is a collection of managed threads usually organized in a queue, which execute the tasks in the task queue. Creating a new thread object every time you need something to be executed asynchronously is expensive. In a thread pool you would just add the tasks you wish to be executed asynchronously to the task queue and the thread pool takes care of assigning an available thread, if any, for the corresponding task. As soon as the task is completed, the now available thread requests another task (assuming there is any left). Thread pool helps you avoid creating or destroying more threads, than would really be necessary.

QUESTION 95: WHAT IS THE DIFFERENCE BETWEEN FAIL-FAST AND FAIL-SAFE IN JAVA?

The Iterator's fail-safe property works with the clone of the underlying collection and thus, it is not affected by any modification in the collection. All the collection classes in **java.util** package are fail-fast, while the

collection classes in **java.util.concurrent** are fail-safe.
Fail-fast iterators throw a
ConcurrentModificationException, while fail-safe iterator
never throws such an exception.

QUESTION 96: WHY ARE ARRAY AND ARRAYLIST DIFFERENT, AND WHEN WOULD YOU USE EACH?

There are some major differences between them.

-An Array is a fixed-length data structure, while
ArrayList is a variable length Collection class. You
cannot change the length of an Array, but
ArrayList can re-size itself. Any resize operation in
an ArrayList slows down performance.

-Array cannot use Generics.

-You cannot store primitives in ArrayLists.

For a list of primitive data types, the collections use
autoboxing to reduce the coding effort. However, this
approach makes them slower when working on fixed size
primitive data types.

QUESTION 97: WHAT IS A JAVA PRIORITY QUEUE?

The PriorityQueue is an unbounded queue, based

on a priority heap and whose elements are ordered in their natural order. At the time of its creation, we can provide a `Comparator` that is responsible for ordering the elements of the `PriorityQueue`. A `PriorityQueue` doesn't allow null values, objects that don't provide natural ordering, or objects that don't have any comparator associated with them. Finally, the Java `PriorityQueue` is not thread-safe and it requires O(log(n)) time for its enqueing and dequeing operations.

QUESTION 98: WHAT IS THE DIFFERENCE BETWEEN ENUMERATION AND AN ITERATOR?

`Enumeration` is twice as fast as compared to an `Iterator` and uses very less memory. However, the `Iterator` is much safer compared to `Enumeration`, because other threads are not able to modify the collection object that is currently traversed by the iterator. Also, `Iterator` tells the caller to remove elements from the underlying collection, something not possible with Enumerations.

QUESTION 99: WHAT IS RENDERSCRIPT? WHEN WOULD YOU USE IT?

`RenderScript` is a scripting language on Android that allows you to write high performance graphic rendering and raw computational code. `RenderScript` provides a means of writing performance critical code that the system later compiles to native code for the processor it can run on. This could be the device CPU, a multi-core CPU, or even the GPU. Which it ultimately runs on depends on many factors that aren't readily available to the developer, but also depends on what architecture the internal platform compiler supports.

QUESTION 100: HOW WOULD YOU PRINT A MESSAGE IN THE LOGCAT AND PREVENT THE APPLICATION FROM STARTING?

```
static {
    System.out.println("Message");
    System.exit(0);
}
```

This code will be executed before the application starts, and then the application will be killed before it has time to start

CAN I ASK YOU FOR A FAVOUR?

If you enjoyed this book, found it useful or otherwise then I'd really appreciate it if you would post a short review on Amazon. I do read all the reviews personally so that I can continually write what people are wanting.

Feedback, typos, questions, doubts, suggestions? Feel free to write me an email to eenriquelopez@gmail.com

Thanks for your support!

www.ingramcontent.com/pod-product-compliance
Lightning Source LLC
Chambersburg PA
CBHW060942050326
40689CB00012B/2546